CH00953288

The 32 Explicit Selected Modern Poems of The Century

With High Technology, Inspirational Credibility

~

Read, Enjoy, Visualize and Analylize

By

Michael M. Chipangura

Copyright © 2016 Michael M. Chipangura Snr

All rights reserved.

ISBN - 10: 1533063958
ISBN - 13: 978-1533063953

DEDICATION

For my family, the beloved children & granddaughters .

CONTENTS

Acknowledgments   vii

Prologue A Line Of Thought – Poem   9

Communication   10
I Dreamed Zimbabwe   11
Politics   13
Who-Who-You Were   14
Meet You Tour   16
Say Sorry   17
Misery Of Gloves   18
Believe Me   19
Best Of Summer Day   20
Invitation   21
Wars   22
The Christmas Eve Light   24
Plane Flight   25
Sun   28
Tragedy   29
Garden View   30
If   31
Desires   32
Wealth Loss   33
Road Network   34
Tears   35
Pride Goes Before A Fall   37
A Marvel   39
Day In Winter   40
No! No - Yes! - Imagine!   41
Nothing To Do   42
At Memorial   43
To Sleep   44
The Infant   45
Name   46
New Year Eve Celebrations   48
Long Life Expectancy   50

ACKNOWLEDGMENTS

I am indebted to all my loved humble children to the nurture and fruition of the book. Of very significance, special importance is to my son- Eusebius Chipangura and his wife Trish. All skilled workers in their jobs who were as hard working on their work as they were on mine for offering enumerable valid variable suggestions and advices to bring the shape, reality and substance to make this Book exist. Its short comings are regrettably all my own.

And, also most grateful, gratitude sincere thanks go to my daughter Yvonne T Chipangura. To my niece Virginia Kufakurova for her endless endurance, commitment, and sacrificed time to type and edit all the superfluous hand written scripts to the final editing and publication of this inspiring Book. I am most so grateful to their great flexible extension of such good skilful crafted hands and ideas. Last but not least, to my undaunted highly spirited wife Theresa T. Chipangura who sacrificed her time day and night approving and disputing countless thoughts and ideas to the fruition of this Fiction Book in spite of her demanding job as a medical nurse at her workplace.

Finally to the Publisher; The Amazon Publishing Company for their understanding and accepting to undergo such mammoth task of work. Without them, the Book wouldn't have come to its full meaning and essence of a worthy readable Book. Once more you are very sincerely, gratefully thanked. 'You are my Hero really worthy the honest faithful praise.'

Amazon My Remarkable Sole Publisher

Amazon Publishing Company, through Create Space has amazingly created a more conducive environment for me to be a writer, and also a successful, very promising author worthy published.
Michael M Chipangura, author of Shona Poem: Ngatidetembanei muTsumo English Poem: Read- Enjoy – Visualize………

Since 1985-6 after attending a Young writers' course at Mount Pleasant and affiliate University of Zimbabwe working complex, I became so incredibly attracted to being both a writer and an effective reader. Being a full time Professional Teacher, that complemented extremely well with my classroom work I so cherished and enjoyed. However, all my other Poem works I sent to Publishing companies in Zimbabwe were of no avail and most discouraged me.

While I continued to and submitted my scripts, I never was published. When I retired in 2012 and came to UK in 2014, I discovered quite remarkable profitable avenues to write and get published. January 2016, I read and researched the Amazon Publishers. 'Here is my only chance to continue to write and have my scripts on the Poems published,' I speculated. So Amazon, through KDP prompted me to be a renowned Author. And, this is just the beginning not the end. Authorship therefor, is and will always be brainstorming me through my life as an author of modern books most acceptable to the present critical, wise, analytical reader as I am.

People may or may not appreciate. Just like love sometimes so hurts, but life always goes on. With Amazon and associates publishers, authorship is broadly perpetuated, and hence publishing with Amazon will accelerate and become one of the most highly recognised predominant publishing establishments in the country, the continent and the world.

'I will get published through Amazon Publishers. It is simple, straightforward, fast and quite efficient.'

Prologue

A LINE OF THOUGHT – POEM

Author of the dreaded past?
No, -yes, know of course,
But of true recent modern present orator all.

That being a writer now,
Cherishes me right grow,
To read and write.

Produce modern today,
Meaningful readable touchy
Poems sensuous glue tight.

Off displeasurable content
But watch, catches human
Mind pleasurable domain.

To think and wonder,
Imagine and portray
Human life in wonder.

Those characteristics thunder,
Actually characterized under
Wonderful world far yonder.

COMMUNICATION

Communication, communication
Communicate life at large
Communicate education this age
Communicate technology the sense.

Then political communication
For economical communication
That business world communication
Then socialization communication.

Communicate transportation
Communicate eviction
Communicate space refutation
Communicate immigration.

Forget not but extracting industry
Remember also secondary industry
And of course not tertiary industry
But target not also services industry.

For
Trade, commercial activities
Communicate, communicate
Communities communicate
Communication skills.

I DREAMED ZIMBABWE

That fascinates fantastic inland
Country of undulating landscape
That snaky, deep valleyed land,
The mountainous engulfs of rifts
Into the glory beauty of the savannas.

Stone brick-work admired
Stone-art work of its in tire
Built of skilful architect
Of no iron, metal nor steel
But yet, only natural granite stone.

Dzimba-dza-mabwe
Original name, so
Name it Zimbabwe
Self-explanatory is Zimbabwe.

Country creedal all natural resources
Self-esteem implore wealth
Agriculture-Mining-Tourisms
All its riches and wealth.

Wealth and riches enhances
Hard productive activities
Concerted efforts to produce
Education opting naïve all services
To the betterment of no individuals.

Seven Wonders of the World
Zimbabwe conveys weird
Attraction tourism best
Lures all mankind the facility
Contribute country economy thrust.

Dreamt dreams Zimbabwe is
Landscape mountainous

Savannah vegetation rifts.
Rich, wealth glorious life Zimbabwean,
I lived in, but dream dreams of Zimbabwe.

POLITICS

That political intimacy of legacy,
That struggle to power
But the rule of law
Of majority legal rights.

Creation rights to live
Nurture right of movement
To right of speech, freedom all,
Basic needs human upkeep
Food-health-shelter-clothes-transport.

The illegal sows,
Political strives to hatred
Purports economic instability
And insecurity to human domination
Country development impeded.

Enhances yes,
Correct corrupt
Looters of wealth
Goes decades unheeded
Well-evil security
Unspurred.

This sparks country unrest,
Results toenails bloodshed
Development to its knees.
Hunger, disease and death prevailed.

So still waters seem,
Don't run deep.
That political intimacy
The socio-economic legacy.

WHO-WHO-YOU WERE

You were enemy and friend
You were rich and poor
You were life and death
You were lost and found
You were love and hate.

You were empty and full
You were man and beast
You were naughty and obedient
You were day and night
You were winter and summer.

You were war and peace
You were wet and dry
You were fat and thin
You were cowardly and courageous.

You were weak and strong
You were dirty and clean
You were sad and happy
You were old and new.

You were east and west
You were south and north
You were deep and shallow
You were failure and success
You were low and high.

You were one legged and two legged
You were two eyed and four eyed
You were nothing and something
You were everywhere and nowhere.

You were who and who
You were now and then
You were negative and positive

You were pessimistic and optimistic
You were remembered and not forgotten
Yes, you were who and who you are.

MEET YOU TOUR

The next morning
I looked at my reflection
Through the bus coach window
Unshaven with that day's paper.

Behind me stood two newspaper men,
Rain muscled its ways through gutters
My past stretches from here to there
And back leaving me, somewhere in the middle
Realized some covetous face different eloquent voice.

Reiterated her name: Toko-E-Annie
Studied Hospitality and Tourism
Harare Poly-narrated her study
And was strained, enabled in the thousand ways of line.

Pleasuring a many line
We shared some shots of wine
With concerted life-talk-fine
Her favourite brand serves a twine.

Knocked them down
And, drank me under table,
Mouth tucked thread to needle,
Hands face and eyes that numb.

Sensuous badly relief,
Hotel room shredded pure
Good warmth off,
Life pays end-memoir tour.

SAY SORRY

Say sorry guy
  You never die
Say sorry
  You never lie.
Say sorry
  Your hands tie
  You have pie
  You never tire.
You have succeeded
You are believed
You are blessed
You are calmed
You are welcomed.
Say sorry; thus:
     You are honoured
     You have soothed
     You have healed
     You have socialized
     You are trusted
   Just say, you are sorry.

MISERY OF GLOVES

Never, they found in singles
Some gloves are loners
They can't live in a pair.

On wash days they have shown us
They want to be loners
They puzzles, confuse their owners.

Hide in dark coins
Surely gloves are loners
They won't live in pairs.

Only on neat-order check
Discover the loner tuck
In wash basket but single
Sure, some gloves are loners.

BELIEVE ME

If you have the way
Then I have got the will
I have the wish.

Let's do what we did
When we did it indeed.

If you have the time
I have got the line
Let's do what we did
When we did it all day
That we did in need.

You got the glass
I have got the wine
We'll do that we did
When we did it overtime.

Sure, time is money
For money is sweet
If you are sure guy
We can do it on our feet
We can do it on the floor
We can do it on the stair
We can do it in the car
We can do it in the air.

If we can do it once a week
We can do it in time
If we can do it once a day
We can do it in a day
If we can do it daily
We can do it hourly
We can do it like we did it
When we did it
That day.

BEST OF SUMMER DAY

Warm summer day
Windows wide open
Lights burning low.

Fruits in bowl flow
Hands shoulder to shoulder hang
Happiest moments tender hug.

Here the late morning hours
Of course, and the time
Just before lunch.

The afternoon,
And evening hours
We closer to one another.

These summers' joys
Ever more, think,
Then those after times.

The work is ended for day.
And no one reaches us then
For never-ever again.

INVITATION

Call at,
    See me sometime
    If my mass is too much for me.

I would have told you
I have lost a kg or no two
    I would have jogged slowly
    I would have weighed low
    I would have scaled more
    I would have run miles slow.

Call at,
    See me sometime;
    But as it is, I'm feeling fine
    Feel no need
    To change my mass
    When I move, fast.

Call at,
    See me sometime;
    Please call my call,
    Sometime call.

WARS

This brutal, under shock monster
Is it love sight of blood-bath,
Or take orders as if oath,
Enjoy-amused use of ammunition
Response-command by superiors
"Take up arms you kill, die or you are killed?"

"Then shalt not kill
Do unto others
As you would like
They do unto you
So chronicles the creator".
Reckon creator's command:
"Love thy neighbour as you love yourself"
'Has it become-of war?

A say   a routine
  A hymn   a pattern
   A litany   a feature
    A norm   and addiction?'
"No! It's a misnomer."

The world over,
The all over
The country wider
The universe over.

Death toll is talk of day
Coupled with disease say
Has inflicted mankind
To misery   to loneliness
  To poverty   to humiliation
   To devastation   to homelessness.

People are murdered like what ever
People are strangled like mice.

People are crushed like whatsoever
People are butchered like animals.
People are maimed like whomever
People are beheaded like criminals.
People are hacked like whosoever
People are shot in cold blood.

Real main course is
Power-power hungry
Greed-greedy of wealth
Corrupt-corrupt of all forms.

Wow!
World coming to an end!
Warned we are,
Take heed,
We are watched.

THE CHRISTMAS EVE LIGHT

Glitter yew city of Harare
Shimmer thither and yonder streets of Harare
Glare, cradle dazzles shine bright above
Trees tall, short and spread wove
Christmas pine trees shine, see
Lights above over all line.

Going the happy love time come,
Of give and take-receive
Gifts of presents no grief
Food, drink and cakes to choices
At table plenty foods dishes
Hear nice love sounds-chats
Of fork-knife and spoon
Enjoy delicious tasty food.

Little ones and loved ones aim
Their happiest time then
Dart-dash and run
Around, thus love the joy-fliers fun
Evening, sparkling trees' streets lights
Explosives colours shot sky high.

Fancy of race games spy laugh
Swing circular or up-down
Of all electrical device operations grown
Ridden and going excitingly
Rhythmic different opposite ways noisily.

Tired and exhausted then pay
Of the activities' day
Parents, children stroll off to cars,
Shove off home to end fares
The spectacular happy bright
Day of Christmas Eve light.

PLANE FLIGHT

Finally the great day came
A plane traditional flight,
Luggage, tickets, rest certified
Correct and in place checked.

Nine thirty pm queue into plane
Soon off Harare airport to UK
Via Lusaka-Zambia
Amsterdam-Holland.

"Fasten your belts, soon taking off"
Monitored instructions,
Zoom-odd sound
I realized, in my
Silence fear of what, how,
Where, next?

Thud throbbed heart sounded
Of fear but excited
Apartment whole in silence dead
Aircraft is hover along
In peaceful lone gear.

Passengers reminded
Of belts tights
Now landing Lusaka
An hour stop spot
With tea-drinks served
Of Air Hostess indeed.

Amsterdam-London
Journey long now
Day getting cool darker
With usual quiet peaceful
Sound, travel aircraft to
Catch up time schedule.

Poor me, sat as still,
Almost a timid lamb
Stiff and numb
Wonder when arrival is.

Inquired whereabouts lo-o
Guided, follow one of the gents
Same missions
Returned meek, with but some relief.

Then stiff steady,
And quiet as usual
Sat as numb silent as statue
T.V before me far off
To any astonishment.

Sure, but are we arriving
Me, myself to no answer
In expectation, serviced lunch
Or was it dinner can't still justify?

"Curiosity killed a cat"
Anxiously, slowly opened a small window
Chilly breezing wind swept across my face
Seemingly, night, turning day
Time read six thirty am.

"Half an hour we should
Touch Heathrow", whispered Theresa
She seemed awake me, no,
For sleep to me, guess what,
Fear and anxiety had taken over.

And sooner or later
Boomed the good news
"Tighten your belts,
Soon landing Heathrow airport
Take all your belongings with you"
Guho-uh-Hu plane landed

Shy-she-she-stopped
The first time in UK
Son and wife, the daughter awaited,
Then
Whisked us home
Wycombe
Bucks
In London
UK.

SUN

Come merry go round
From where go,
East-West-East
Or South-North South
Is it rotate revolve
Or revolve-rotate?

Who would then know?
You sun wouldn't.
None from of where little thoughts
But a merry goes around
Rotate-revolve.

Stifle brain deep
Of young and old
Beyond comprehend
Sunlight begets darkness,
But where are you?

Like a vicious cycle
Repeated goes light
Darkness comes
Come warmth old go
Beyond Meer human ego,

For none to the core
Gained the grasp of your circles
Only you, know the incredible
Where come, -go. The usual issue
Merry –go round- rotate or revolve.

TRAGEDY

I crawled from the noise of upturn truck
Silence in dark began to grow.
I called on him repeatedly
To where neither life nor move, come
World no but answer none.

Attended funeral with fear grieved
Reflected no home of homes this pain
Without him life couldn't bear anymore
Yes, that was less than one trance vein
Unspeakable devastation life-shock.

The shock memory of
Truck lie on its roof
Trail of flow Blood Street,
Eyes of fear hesitant scare
Crowd with anguish shout
Shame life unpleasant –gone
Perish and death is grief.

Disgust memories of lone sleep
But snares of what life real is
My future-lone spectacular be
That he gone never ever
Again in sight, but memories
Of agony miss misery ever home
Dwell loner a Habitat so sore.

GARDEN VIEW

Come through the gate and feast your feel
With garden created by someone wise, tell
Of beautiful flower garden all scented smell,
Expressing wonder of flowers roses mellow
To artistic rows assorted grow well.

Stroll and bask the sunshine warmth
Insects busy, nectar-pollen collect,
Sweet juicy food to their grubs.
Squirrels twitch-jump-dart across to
A busy, thicket trees tall and leafy.

Feast eyes with greenish attractive
Vegetables bench-marked space
To allow nature of sunlight
Warm ingredients success
Yield to plenty food and for trade.

And for many passer-by's,
Admire organised displays
Of proper intensely use,
Given natural resources
To productive small tourist, botanic
Museum garden attribute to organics
Come, feast your eyes, and go through the garden
gate.

IF

If I were you,
       I would smile
       And run a mile
       In a while.

If I were you,
       I wouldn't strain
       My brain
       With pain.

If I were you,
       I would budget
       For a gadget
       Not a reject.

If I were you,
       I wouldn't laugh
       A cough
       So rough.

If I were you,
       I would care
       For a fare
       That is fair.

If I were you,
       I would buy a reasonable
       Nice table
       That is portable.

If I were you,
       I would rejoice
       With a sweet voice
       For better choice.
If I were you,
       I wouldn't hesitate
       To evaluate
       As to isolate
None of those
If I were you.

DESIRES

He desires he were an imp
With subjects of his own all round
And penetrated the thickets beastly dangers
Enthroned glitter commando robes on him.

He desires he were a warrior chief commander,
A fearless powerful soldier all dreadful
With army carrying weaponry deadly
Such warrior safe to wage a strong war.

And desired wishes of a drummer chief imp
To beat upon a drum sound to alert
And hear the crowd all shouts
Watch, see there, imp warrior race along.
Dead, we all, gone ancestors home buried.

WEALTH LOSS

Explore rumoured diamond fields,
Tour the cradle districts rich lands
Believed of wealthy stones glitters
Richness of fields' milk, and honey
Promised land of plenty by state.

Precious stones are real
Diamond ornamental products
Shall glitter, hold shops heavy,
To country-trade swells foreigners
Customers from every world corner.

Indigenous jealousy rage, conspires snares
Amongst themselves groups corrupt
Activities to strained state security,
But looters converge more,
To stealthily smuggle out off.

Own wealth and richness where to-
Harboured unknown secrete destiny,
Again render people unemployed and
Wonder the given rich fortune all in vain
Poverty, hunger and disease overcome homes.

What a societal curse!
Can't hardly be explained, even by economists
Unable to provide enough data with
Unbelievable trend of events that occurred,
Leaving analysts dumb-trodden, anguish
And, but; crying foul.

ROAD NETWORK

My trunk road leads to Harare - Marsh North
One trunk road runs to Byo –Mat -South
Other roads lead me to Gweru-Mid -Central
Many, while drift through link towns to Mutare – Manicaland.

One trunk road leads to the largest dam
Now known as Zimbabwe Great Lake
As if meanders along gorgeous slow, River-Zambezi
There, fish industry booms, the country
Supply food and export looms, and, to
Satisfy the fish men goals.

Most lead me, lure me, attract and call me
To blue, green tossing massive lake waters,
To vegetation green thickets, savannah of Eastern Highlanders
Trunk roads without earth's road dust
Are the clear right roads for all to use.

Many satisfy motorists travel safe
To West, East, South and North
Most trunk roads lead to many Tourist Attraction sites.
After enjoyment of some wonders of
The country sceneries ever
Some reckoned renown as of over
The World, wonders of the World.

TEARS

Tears factor is
Tears of joy
Tears of sorrow
Tears of sadness and
Tears of happiness.

Tears fall in time of joy
When extreme happiness
Prevails, sharing at
Weddings and birthdays' parties
Loved ones memoir occasions.

Tears run down our cheeks,
Release tensions in Times
Unpredictable success results announced,
Celebrate with relatives, friends and neighbours
Converge to praise roused pride emotions joy
With sweet music sound, blend it all.

Love grieved tears of
Facial joy trickles down,
Silent sob cry to;
Prestigious gifts express, hug good bye
When part to meet in all happiness.

Tears are shed real
In loss of loved ones pale
By events of sad deaths-arrests
Or imprisoned for life say,
Rouse emotions of despair.

Perceived by those reassured
Responsibility in care,
Triggers pervasive emotional
Touch of heat towards gloomy
State-life experience-pain
With desperation.

To reflex tears of endless joy and
Imminent bitter sorrow.

PRIDE GOES BEFORE A FALL

Pride goes before a fall
And fall comes before pride
Life comes, goes pride and fall
Life is struggle and stumble.

You, me everyone
Here, there everywhere
In, out within or without
Pride goes before a fall.

On land-in by air
In or under water
In space- space- crafts
Pride goes before a fall.

Gamble yes, but not with
Life regrets you will
Feature with in life
But non ridicule exposure jubilation.

Impress candid wealth
Acquired but in honest
For suppress to amass riches'
Thus stifles, deprives others' life-flow.

Implore corrupt, entice activities
Down trodden populous progress
Country, to its knees, poverty-stricken
And disease-hunger-befriend.

Hunger begets war tactics
Befriend death as is hunger to disease
Stop measure is difficult control
A big glow of fire higher rolls.

Gamble yes, but not with
Life regret you will

Life comes, goes pride and fall
For pride goes before a fall.

A MARVEL

Material-matter for use
God creator facilitated
Man-animal to use
Living non-living by the creator
Creatures great and small
Made use for ever marvel.

Human brain more matter to marvel
Human intellect obstinate marvel
Human sensuous incredible a marvel
Human technical abilities how a marvel
Human manipulates material-matter
Hush a marvel.

Incredible fantastic technology.
None-ever but dreams come true,
Press button this end,
Respond an answer the opposite end.
Message this end, the other response.
Write, draw whatever, whichever end
The other end reflects recapitulates.

Near or far
Over and above, under
Land or space,
Above water or under water
Solid or perforated walls,
The human intellect technology
Unabated easily sails through.

The waves control catch ups,
The electronics technical know-how
The sensuous human intelligent operations
Whole manifestation (technical) skills
Marvels human beliefs.
Incredible, fantastic passionate discovery
To easy communications concerns.

DAY IN WINTER

Weather forecast warned stern,
Severe cold winter weather approach
The merciless wretched winter snowfall
Now here then.

Snow covered streets as slut
Pavement capped flat
Melted snow hidden lumps
Combined with mud to slush.

Thick fog called street lights
Traffic impeded rest
Slip or gild impassable roads
People room-bound tucked in warm garments.

Long sunsets or sunrises invisible
Clouds hung low over sky
Either grey or mud colours
Dropping heavy rainy drops.

Hail stones hit, sound scary
A four o'clock noon confuses
Daylight was ended
With electricity-gas exhaustion.

Adults and children huddle,
Wrapping themselves up in
Thick-fur warm clothes
Expectancy of an improved day.

Incessant rain-chilly breezes
Dreadful drizzle and fog smells
In streets and pavements people
Scuttle and waddle along.

The persistence unknown
In the mirrors
And who knows

Perhaps same sorrows.

NO! NO - YES! - IMAGINE!

Hey!-Hush-Wharf
No sun- no moon- no day
No moon- a noon- any night
No down- no dash- no proper time of day
No sky- no earthly view
No distance looking blue.

No road- no street- no path
No subway- no rail- no railway
No carriage way- no tunnel- no bridge
No pipe- no drainages
No sight of those in place.

No cart- no bicycle- no car
No motor-bike- no motorcycle
No train- no aeroplane
No boat- no ship- no canoe
No space-craft- no universe explores.

No medicine- no nurse- no doctor
No hospital- no patient- no disease
No scientist- no physician- no pharmacist
No experiment- no education- no success
No life- no reproduction- no existence.

No company- no nobility
No laugh- no cheers – no happiness
No relative- no friendship- no sadness.

No media- no news- no communication
No sight of any familiar living thing.
No nothing of anything nowhere something.

Hey! Hush! Wharf

No! - Yes! - Imagine!

NOTHING TO DO

Having nothing to do – you are joking
With nothing to do – you are lying
Having nothing to do – you are playing
With nothing to do – you are lazing.

Joking, you will, when you take shows
Lying, you will, when you exaggerate chats
Playing, you will, when day is rest
Lazing, you will, when you stop, think,
Loitering, you will, when you are free.

Having nothing to do is short lived
With nothing to do is infamous
Having nothing to do is infernal
With nothing to do is disgrace
Having nothing to do is mischief.

Having nothing to do is hostile
With nothing to do is cynic
Having nothing to do is curse
With nothing to do is falsehood
Having nothing to do is fallacy
Having nothing to do is all fraud.

Unacceptable,
Unreasonable,
Insensible,
Inconvincible,

All is fraud incredible having nothing to do.

AT MEMORIAL

Many spoke highly of her
Ostentations beauty fades away
Passionate moralist display
Truthful, faithful receptionist humour
No one heard the sobbing angle lower.

I lived her life and she lived mine
Will have my own weeping to do,
Not only in the valleys of deceit,
But also in honest of waters
Where no word is singular.

Uphill road to happiness
Speed limits the traffic easy flow
Uphill-down hill road bumpy
Gone as cloud float by, she;
Now lies in peace but no rest.

That marriage life-tie untie off,
The gloomy of it all in death
God put to call, we can't complain,
Accept in it, meek,
Never will it,
Ever again mend.

TO SLEEP

A call of no command
Supervised by none, but
Nurtures its way.

In colour night gowns worn
Lie in warm neat bed that comforts
Activities stay, put reinforces.

Trigger on gun goes near
Dream sleep surprises who,
The glory of deep-lovely sleep hears.

Spectacular splendours' silent deep
Sleep of none commands, but so cheap
Expect dream, unconscious dreams dreamt.

THE INFANT

Welcome you
The expectancy
Of the unknown
Now comes this world.

Welcome unconfined
Now you real home
You little fingers-toes
Clutch-stretch open
In beauty of new life.

Celebration occasion come
Bring gifts of joy rejoice
Of all sorts-colours
Bright and beautiful welcome you.

Rejoice by imminent dances
Of excellence celebration expedience
By music rhyme unison
Release-hold hands to
Legs combined slight step-jump.

Birthday party nowhere
Baby that you now crown
The modest of mother, father
Love you yes your parents rejoice
Welcome to your real royal home.

Rejoice and be grown, enclosures
You will be everywhere
But nowhere life to come
That distinguished welcome, to
New royal home baby
New baby respect intense that welcome.

NAME

It's Africa.
It's America.
It's Churumanzu.
It's Zimbabwe.

I am Chisadza.
I am Chipangura
I am James.
I am Victoria.

Kudzai is my name.
John is my name.
Grace is my name.
Tsitsi is my name.
Name it:
A stick
Wind
A man
An insect.

"It is a name of anything"
Something unique in name
Something extraordinary in name
Something meaning in name
Something peculiar in name.

In it all:
Name tells one's background
Name depicts one's culture
Name resembles one's tradition
Name invokes one's origin

Name it: Name
Its' a noun
A name of anything with a meaning.

Expressing
Virtues
And
Values.

Virtues
And
Values through thought, word and habits.

NEW YEAR EVE CELEBRATIONS

Spectacular glamorous displays,
Of gorgeous fireworks uniquely glow rocket high,
Illuminate spectrum vast, immense area
City attractive to communities of all races.

Spacious fireworks shot spiky bursts missiles like,
Into sky to crimson colours about,
Geometric gestures all directions scenes
Twilight spread circles, sideways scenery dazzles.

Triangular, octagonal, circulars splash,
And, like rockets, burst- flash countless
Directions catch spectators' eyes glued,
To flickering, fizzle crackle bounded sound.

Fantastic beautiful- nice crimson colours meander,
And crack- flash like thunder on,
Stormy hours with clouds row race now,
Produce smoky scattered pointer missiles.

Of, like rainbow, hear the crinkle cracking
Sound in unison rhythmic style.
Feverish crowds in emotions imitate
Amicable, glory music of new life –New Year.

Accelerate bands of acrobatic musical artists
So selected to complement the momentous
Special events with eminent known
Traditional and cultural life variations.

Feverish crowds screech in amazing emotional joy
Ululating explicit songs of mutual joy sorrow.
Breeze, cold weather conditions over-taken by
Jump, up, down and sway or hoping jubilation,

Melodically music and dance entwined in touchy
Many a crowds, well familiarized,
To the tingle of big ben watch, then,

Acentric accelerated amusement and happiness.

Shout in thunderous jubilation;
Happy a new year
Come 2015 come
With all plenty.
A spectacular prosperous 2015.
Peace and tranquil, we ask
God's guidance, we admire
Christ's revelation, we implore
With all blessings.

LONG LIFE EXPECTANCY

Guess, it never does
Guard it yes, urged
As closely as is impossible
By reflex relentless exercises.

Diet guide of course
Guard against sugary foods
Fats promote energy warmth
Cholesterol free bid yes.

Reduce carbohydrates foods
But of roughage moderate,
Vegetable sparingly taken, consume
All but vitamin A, B recommended.

Less liquids drinks,
No sugar added access
But protein reassure
Vitamins, the major three
Doctor's visits routines.

Advice medication, nod regular
Gymnasium exercises lacks
Physical tissue organs strain
Operate adhere to really
Ensure life pace,
Long Expectancy
Through dietary and exercises are advise

About The Author

Michael M Chipangura was born in 1945. Second May. He is the last born of the ten children in the family. He pioneered Chikwingwizha Secondary school in 1961. Presently he is a retired professional teacher after qualifying at Bondolfi Teacher's College in Masvingo in 1966. He stays in Harben Park at No 39 Morgan Road in Gweru. Mr M Chipangura currently lives in the United Kingdom where he is actively pursuing his passion of writing poems & stories. Mr Chipangura, from 1967 taught at various Primary Schools in Zimbabwe in the senior section for more than forty years.

In 1985-86, the interest and enthusiasm to become a writer was more triggered when he attended a Young writer's course at Mount Pleasant, an affiliate programme of The University of Zimbabwe (UZ) Harare.

The late Professor Dr Solomon Mangwiro Mutsvairo and Professor Micere Githae Mugo led and conducted the panellists into the discussion sessions. It was here during his holidays when he became attracted into being an inspiring writer. At the end of the sessions, he produced some quite remarkable Poems in Shona and English. Some that are read and benefits the Zimbabwean child at different many Primary schools particularly in Midlands Region today.

Thanks and most grateful to Dr S. M. Mutsvairo and Professor M. G. Mugo for stimulating and inspiring him to be a productive good author. Also most grateful thanks and appreciation go to the panelists as well as participants during the busy profitable course.

Printed in Great Britain
by Amazon

82148877R00029